DAVID A. ADLER

The Number on My Grandfather's Arm

UAHC Press · New York, New York

Family photographs by Rose Eichenbaum
Photos on pages 13, 15, and 19 courtesy Yad Vashem

Feldman Library

THE FELDMAN LIBRARY FUND was created in 1974 through a gift from the Milton and Sally Feldman Foundation. The Feldman Library Fund, which provides for the publication by the UAHC of selected outstanding Jewish books and texts, memorializes Sally Feldman, who in her lifetime devoted herself to Jewish youth and Jewish learning. Herself an orphan and brought up in an orphanage, she dedicated her efforts to helping Jewish young people get the educational opportunities she had not enjoyed.

In loving memory of my beloved wife Sally
"She was my life, and she is gone;
She was my riches, and I am a pauper."

"Many daughters have done valiantly,
but thou excellest them all."

Milton E. Feldman

This is my grandfather.
He listens when I talk,
and he answers all my questions.

Grandpa is a tailor.
Whenever I tear a blouse or skirt,
Grandpa fixes it.
When I grow and my skirts are too short,
Grandpa makes them longer.

When Grandpa was young,
he lived in a small village
in Eastern Europe.
I asked Grandpa about the village
and he told me, "It was in the mountains.
There was a lake near us.
I swam in it with my friends."

Grandpa also told me, "We had no cars.
We traveled in wagons pulled by horses.
But we didn't travel much,
just to the next village."

"Did you have brothers and sisters?" I asked.
"Yes," Grandpa said. "But they're gone.
They're dead," he said softly.
"My friends are gone, too."

Grandpa lives in this building,
in his own apartment.
But he visits us a lot.
He usually wears a necktie and jacket.
Sometimes, in the summer,
he takes off his jacket.
But even when it's hot,
Grandpa always wears a long-sleeved shirt.

One night my parents were going out.
Grandpa came over after supper to be with me.
He saw my parents were in a hurry
so he said he'd wash the dishes.
Grandpa took off his jacket and necktie.
He rolled up the sleeves of his shirt,
and I saw a number on his arm.

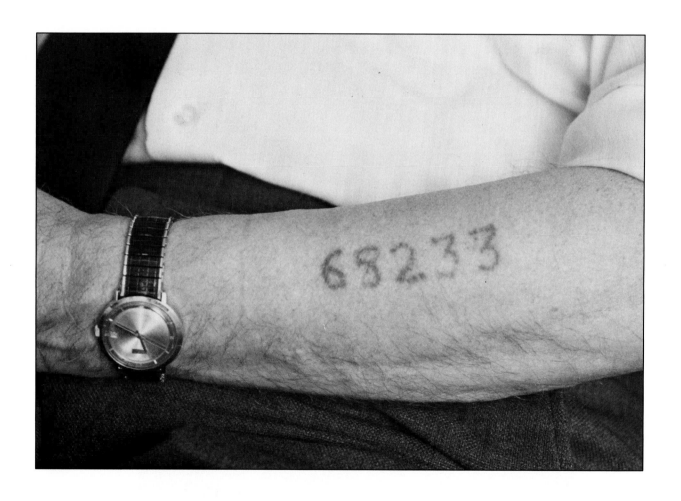

"What's that?" I asked.
Grandpa quickly folded his arms.
The number was hidden.
"What's that?" I asked again.

Grandpa looked at my mother.
She spoke softly.
"It's time you told her," she said.
Grandpa rolled down his sleeves.
He put on his jacket and
walked into the living room.

I followed Grandpa
and sat next to him on the couch.
"I'll tell you about the number," Grandpa said.
He was speaking softly, too.
It was hard to hear every word he said.

"I was born in Europe, in Poland.
When I was young, I studied in school.
I played with my friends,
with my brothers and sisters.
But terrible things were happening
outside our village.

"Adolf Hitler was the ruler of Germany then.
He was a wild man.
He waved his arms and shouted about the Jews.
And, when he shouted,
thousands of people shouted, too.

"There were a great many problems in Germany.
Hitler blamed them all on the Jews.
Of course that was nonsense.
But the German people were happy
to blame someone—
even if it wasn't true.
Jews lost their jobs and their homes.
Signs all over Germany said,
'Jews not wanted here.'
Hitler's soldiers kicked Jews,
made fun of us.
Jews were forced to wear a yellow star.
They were beaten and killed.
Synagogues were destroyed.
In other countries, too,
in Italy, Hungary, Austria, Yugoslavia,
and in my Poland,
people all talked about how they hated the Jews."

"That's terrible," I said.
"It got worse," Grandpa told me.

"Hitler and his Nazi soldiers
planned to take over all of Europe.
With planes, guns, bombs, and tanks
they conquered one country after another.
In each country they killed Jews.
Hitler and the Nazis planned to kill
every Jew in Europe.

"They built concentration camps.
Millions of Jews
were forced into those camps.
Others were brought there, too.
The Nazis called us all 'enemies of the state.'
I was in one of them, Auschwitz.
It was surrounded with a high fence.
On top of that fence was barbed wire.
There were guards with guns.
There was no way out of that camp.

"In Auschwitz they printed numbers on our arms.
We were no longer people to them.
We were numbers.

"The Nazis hardly fed us.
They tortured us.
And they killed us.
The Nazis killed
six million Jewish men, women, and children
—innocent people.
Some were my friends, my family."

There were tears in Grandpa's eyes
and in my eyes, too.

"I was one of the lucky ones," Grandpa said.
"I survived."

We just sat there for a while.
We didn't talk.
I imagined what it was like for Grandpa
to be in that concentration camp.
It must hurt him to remember
the time he spent there
and to remember all the people he knew
who were killed.

After we sat there for a long while,
I put my hand on Grandpa's and told him,
"You shouldn't be ashamed
to let people see your number.
You didn't do anything wrong.
It's the Nazis who should be ashamed."

Grandpa hugged me.
Then he looked at me and smiled.
He wiped away his tears and said,
"Let's take care of those dishes now."

Grandpa went into the kitchen again.
He took off his jacket
and rolled up his sleeves.
He washed the dishes,
and I dried them.

David A. Adler is the author of more than sixty books, including *Our Golda: The Story of Golda Meir*, selected as an Outstanding Social Studies Book by the Children's Book Council, and *A Picture Book of Jewish Holidays*, chosen as a Notable Book by the American Library Association. He is also the author of the popular *Cam Jansen* series.

Rose Eichenbaum, the photographer of the family pictures for the book, has been occupied during much of her professional career with children's portraiture. The daughter of Holocaust survivors, she now lives in Los Angeles with her husband Betzalel and their three children. Seven-year-old *Ariella*, the Eichenbaum's eldest daughter, is the child in the photos in *The Number on My Grandfather's Arm*.

Sigfried Halbreich, the grandfather in *The Number on My Grandfather's Arm*, a Polish-born Holocaust survivor, helped the U.S. War Crimes Branch prepare for the Nuremberg trials. He has testified at the trials of Nazi criminals including the trial of Adolf Eichmann. He now lives in Beverly Hills, California.